Little Wisdom

Sumayyah

ISBN: 0615869955
ISBN-13: 978-0615869957

Cover by AMB Branding and Design

Photography by Eric Muhammad

DEDICATION

To all the kids with big dreams

ACKNOWLEDGMENTS

I would like to thank Allah for my gifts.

Thanks to my mom and dad for their love.

Thanks to my siblings, Miss Angie, Ms. Suzanne, Ms. Lynell and Sister Mary Alice for helping me along the way with learning.

Thanks to my friend Alika for being a great friend. I miss you.

Young African Americans

Attention young African Americans

We should be free to do whatever and
whomever we want to be.

Our lives should be fed and not starved.

Our lives should be safe and not dangerous

And most of all, our lives should be free.

We should stand up and have confidence

Speak up for who we are

Stand up

Family

We all should have confidence and faith in ourselves and each other.

We have everything we need in each one of us…all over the world

There are three special words that make it happen:

Passion, love and religion.

Everyone has a family.

Everyone wants a family.

Everyone needs a family.

Family, success, passion, love, career, education, and religion

We need all of these in order to survive.

Without these things, our lives will be deserted without hope.

Trayvon Martin

Trayvon Martin was a great person

He didn't deserve to be shot

He was shot at the age of seventeen

He will never grow up

He will never have a little girl like me.

Trayvon Martin was killed by George Zimmerman

Because he was black

George Zimmerman was found not guilty

We all have support for Trayvon Martin and his parents

You will be missed and love by many.

Why I Love Horses

I love horses because they are fun

You can ride them: English or western style

You can groom their shiny coat

And even compete in shows with them

Horses have a different relationship with you than people

They have good and bad ones

If you love your horse, they will love you.

You don't like them, they will know it.

Horses make great friends for kids like me.

Pennsylvania Horse Show where I won two-first place and overall champion ribbons

The Environment

The environment is nice and big
There are many things to do and see
There are many resources around us
Such as trees and plants
They help us with the things we use every day
It is important to keep it clean and safe
Not just for our health but because we will not
Have a lot of things without it.
Let's work together to keep it safe
For people and animals.

Happiness

Happiness shows fun and laughter

It means making friends and being friends

Happiness is friendship and love

It makes everyone happy

It makes you happy and everyone else around you

Happiness can be passed on from one person to another

Get happy today!

Love

Love is about family and friends

Love shows courage and confidence

It makes people come together

And spread love to other people

Love is all around the world

I love people around the country

And you should too.

Daddy

My daddy and I have fun

We wrestle and build stuff together

Fathers can teach you how to ride a bike

Or read a book

They can teach and help you with anything

Fathers love you no matter what and always will

Having a father is very special

I love my daddy.

Mommy

My mommy is sweet and fun

Mothers can teach you how to read and write

How to be pretty and love yourself

Mothers can teach you different things than a father can

They love you more than anything else in the world

I love my mommy very much.

Best Friends

Friends form different relationships than your family

They help you like friends should do

They comfort you when you are sad

And make you laugh

They make you feel good inside with pride

There is nothing like having one good friend

You can make friends with people all over the world.

My friend Alika is nice and funny

We play together and have lots of fun

We help each other when we're feeling down or get hurt

We have had some good and bad times together

That's what being best friends is about.

Wealth

Wealth isn't always about being rich and famous

It's about sharing and helping other people

Yes, we need it to get food and energy and stuff for our daily needs

Without it, we wouldn't be able to live long.

Wealth means different things to different people

You can be wealthy in love or life and not have money

Money isn't the most important thing in the world

But you are.

Reading

Reading is important in everyone's lives

It helps you learn

We use reading to understand directions, books and signs

You are never too old to learn how to read

It is something that everyone must learn

It helps you do things in your daily life

Reading is everywhere

Reading is fun

Reading is important.

The Sun

The sun rises in the day and sets at night

When the sun shine son the earth, it is daylight

The sun is bright and hot

But it is also good for our bodies

It gives us energy

It gives us life

It shines around the world

It warms the earth

I hope it never stops shining on the world.

Death

Death is sad and frightening

Death can happen in many different ways

You never know how much it hurts to lose someone until they die

You may cry or be angry

It is not a good feeling

We pray for the family of those who die

When people die, they are no longer suffering or hurting

Take care of yourself so you can live a long time.

Loving Yourself

Loving yourself is taking care of yourself

Love yourself no matter what

Taking care of yourself is something you should do everyday

Loving yourself is hugging yourself

When you love yourself, you tell others that you love them as well.

Loving yourself is loving the skin you are in

Loving yourself isn't other people's business

No one can tell you how to love yourself

You have to figure that out

Love yourself just the way you are.

Life

In life, some things are the same

Some things are different

When things change, we don't always like them

Change is not easy

It takes time to do things in a different way than we are used to.

Always do your best

You have it inside you to do the best you can with everything you do.

No one can stop you but you

No matter who you are or what you do, always remain to be you.

Kwanzaa brings black families together

It runs from December 26th to January 1st every year

Red, black and green represents us

Red stands for the blood of our people

Black stands for our people

Green stands for the land of Africa

There are seven principles in Kwanzaa

Umoja, Kujichagulia, Ujima, Ujamaa, Nia, Kuumba, Imani

Every day a candle is lit

There is food, song, poems and dance

Such a great celebration.

Beautiful natural me

As pretty as I can be

I'm happy

I love who I am

I love who I have become

I am comfortable in my own skin

I feel good

I feel liked. I feel love.

I feel unique

I am beautiful natural me.

My favorite horse….Polar Bear

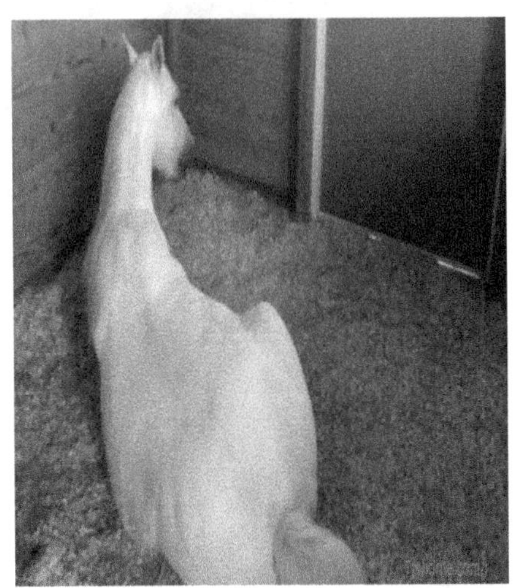

Leave your own inspirational words on this page.

www.ingramcontent.com/pod-product-compliance
Lightning Source LLC
LaVergne TN
LVHW010550100826
845148LV00013B/2677

* 9 7 8 0 6 1 5 8 6 9 9 5 7 *